Xenophobe's®
guide to the
FRENCH

Nick Yapp
Michael Syrett

G000321022

Oval Books

Published by Oval Books

Telephone: +44 (0)20 7733 8585
Fax: +44 (0)20 7733 8544
E-mail: info@ovalbooks.com

Published by Ravette Publishing, 1993
Reprinted/updated: 1994,1995,1996,1997,1998

Published by Oval Books, 1999
Reprinted: 2000, 2001
Updated 2002, reprinted 2003
Updated 2004, 2005, 2006
Reprinted 2007
New edition 2008

Series Editor – Anne Tauté

Cover designer – Jim Wire & Vicki Towers
Printer – J H Haynes & Co Ltd, Sparkford
Producer – Oval Projects Ltd

Xenophobe's® is a Registered Trademark.

Thanks are given to Michael England
for his help and information.

ISBN: 978-1-906042-32-5

Contents

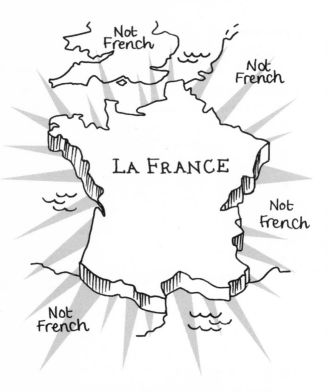

'The French see brilliance in everything they do, and French statesmen from the Renaissance to de Gaulle and on to Chirac have likened France herself to a guiding light.'

The French population is 62 million – compared with 42 million Spanish, 52 million English, 58 million Italians, 82 million Germans and 303 million Americans.

Nationalism & Identity

Forewarned

The French care about what really matters in life – being French. They care more about doing everything with enormous style than about what they do. They are convinced of their corporate and individual superiority over all others in the world. Their charm is that they don't despise the rest of us: they pity us for not being French.

The notion of '*la force*' lies at the heart of everything the French have done, well or badly, in the last thousand

> **66 Their charm is that they don't despise the rest of us: they pity us for not being French. 99**

years or more. *La force* is their sense of the essence of life. It is bound up with other grand ideas such as '*la gloire*' and '*la patrie*', feminine words that speak of boundless stores of energy. The French are attracted to all things vibrant, alive, moving, irresistible. Beneath their chic and natty appearances they respond to atavistic and primitive impulses.

Where most other nations would be embarrassed or appalled by the notion of the thinly veiled body of Marianne (the symbol of the Republic) leaping over the barricades, musket in hand, the French are moved to tears of real patriotism. The cockerel may well be their national symbol – a colourful male bird that makes a great deal of noise, chases off all rivals and lays no eggs – but they never forget that their country is *la* France.

This is why they are a sensual people: who kiss where others shake hands; who proudly say that they make love in the same way that they eat; who write music that sounds like the sun rising out of the sea. And it's also why they are so concerned with appearances, taking seven and a half minutes to wrap a small *tarte aux cerises* – putting it in a box, tying it with ribbon and handing it to the customer as though it were a new-born baby – when the blessed thing is going to be consumed the moment it's taken out of the *pâtisserie*.

> **They are a public, unembarrassed people, made for special occasions – banquets, weddings, festivals, fêtes.**

They are a public, unembarrassed people, made for special occasions – banquets, weddings, festivals, fêtes. Here they perform, happy in their roles and the overall production. In their homes, they are too cabined, cribbed, confined. The settings in which they are best seen are offices, restaurants, airport lounges (who else looks good in these?) opera houses, *grands boulevards*. They may sometimes behave badly, but they always act superbly.

How they see themselves

The French see themselves as the only truly civilised people in the world. Long ago they discovered the

2

absolutes, the certainties of life, and thus they feel they have a duty to lead and illuminate the rest.

On anything that matters they consider themselves experts. Anything in which they are not experts does not matter. All life, all energy, is a grand force of nature, which they embrace whole-heartedly. They see glory in what others regard as defeat. Since they have won almost every war they have entered, they assume that the final battle must have resulted in a French victory. Because of this, those who visit England and happen to travel through Waterloo Station won-

> **❝ Their role in relation to the rest of the world borders on the Messianic. ❞**

der why the British named it after a battle they lost.

They also see honour in seduction, triumph in a well-cooked entrecôte, and world supremacy in a bottle of *grand cru*. Not for nothing was Louis XIV called 'the Sun King', for the French see brilliance in everything they do, and French statesmen from the Renaissance to de Gaulle and on to Chirac have likened France herself to a guiding light. Their role in relation to the rest of the world borders on the Messianic.

How they see others

To give their own feeling of superiority some validity, the French are generously prepared to accept that

3

other nations have to exist. But do not expect the French to be 'politically correct' in anything they do. They can be racist, chauvinistic and xenophobic, but always with great charm, and whereas the English would feel guilty for having such sentiments, the French believe that it's natural.

They find the Spanish proud but noisy, and believe they produce more wine than is healthy for the vineyards of the Midi. Spanish wine may be sub-standard to the tastebuds of the French, but '*ça existe*' – an ominous phrase.

> **66** They find the Spanish proud but noisy, and believe they produce more wine than is healthy for the vineyards of the Midi. **99**

They see the English as small-minded, uncultured, faintly ridiculous, badly dressed; a nation of people who spend most of their time gardening, playing cricket and drinking thick, sweet, warm beer in pubs. Yet they remain curious about them. They may refer to English day-trippers to Calais as '*les fuck-offs*' and still regard the British generally as '*perfide*' (because the French jury is still out on the little matter of whether or not Napoleon was poisoned while on St. Helena), but after one glass of Scottish malt whisky, much is forgiven.

The French don't dislike the Germans but they are not fond of them. They are willing to acknowledge their industrial supremacy but regard their culture as inferior to their own. This is not discrimination. In

4

their view, every other culture is inferior to their own.

They also feel politically superior to the Germans since the Germans lost all international 'presence' when they were stripped of their colonies after the First World War. The French may no longer own much of the world, but French law, language and culture persist in every continent.

Despite their reservations and however uncomfortable they find the thought, the French have much in common with the Germans – a sense of formality, a reserve, a concept of racial purity, a belief in an historical destiny.

> **"Despite their reservations, the French have much in common with the Germans, however uncomfortable they find the thought."**

The exceptions to this admiring–despising axis are the Belgians and the Swiss. The Swiss are objects of merciless satire in French television commercials. They may be hospitable, but they are obsessively clean and speak French in a most odd fashion.

Valuing style in everything they do, the French have nothing but contempt for the Belgians, who they see as universally dull and totally lacking in finesse. To the French, the Belgians have always been *bête*, 'thick', and they are the butt of an endless stream of French jokes, e.g:

Two Belgian soldiers are sleeping under a tree.
Suddenly a terrible rumbling sound awakes them.
'Hell and death,' says the first. 'A storm!'

'No,' says the other, 'those are bombs.'

'Thank God for that,' says the first. 'I'm terrified of thunder.'

A little envy has crept into these jokes now that the French realise the Belgians have a better standard of living than they do.

Special relationships

Historically, the French have had a special relationship with the United States and Canada, having owned much of the former and populated much of the latter. But complications have arisen. When a French film is shown at a French-Canadian cinema it has to have subtitles because the Canadians cannot understand the soundtrack, their accent is so different.

The French have long admired the Americans – for their constitution (based on the French), for their code of law (based on the French), and for kicking out the English. Yet they go to considerable lengths to stave off the corrupting influence of American culture – restricting the number of American fast-food outlets, limiting imports of U.S. goods, and dumping EuroDisney sufficiently far from Paris to give it a sporting chance of failure. Curiously, the French have successfully persuaded generation after generation of Americans to fall in love with them, without reciprocating that love.

How others see them

The trouble with the French, in the eyes of many, is that they are inconsistent. This is because others fail to see that the French decide all big issues on the basis of self-interest, a feature of peasant ideology.

This trait is to be seen in all aspects of French life. They exasperate with their ox-drawn, lumbering approach to the delights of a market economy, but exhilarate with their Quixotic flights of fancy in some international projects. They produce the most beautiful paintings in the world and the ugliest wallpaper. They grow the finest vegetables and never serve them in their restaurants. If anything goes

> **66 They produce the most beautiful paintings in the world and the ugliest wallpaper. 99**

wrong with the heating or air-conditioning on one of their trains, three uniformed *conducteurs* will visit each compartment apologising profusely (*"nous sommes désolés…"*), yet these same *conducteurs* will cheerily slam the coach doors shut in your face as you race to get on board.

They work hard, but are never seen to be working. Drive through France at any time of the day, week, month or year and 95% of the country appears to be uninhabited or fast asleep.

What others need to understand is that the French regard consistency as boring, and to be boring is inexcusable.

How they would like others to see them

Since the French are so full of their own self-esteem, they don't really care how others see them.

Character

The essential Frenchman

It is every Frenchman's secret wish to be Cyrano de Bergerac, the braggart, swaggering hero of Edmund Rostand's play. Cyrano, like d'Artagnan, was a Gascon: sensitive yet strong; a great swordsman, but also a poet of infinite tenderness; a passionate lover,

> **66 It is every Frenchman's overt wish to be Gérard Depardieu. 99**

yet one who died of the greatest unrequited love in all literature; a man who failed, but failed gloriously. And what most endears Cyrano to all Frenchmen is that, to the end, he maintained his *panache*.

It is every Frenchman's overt wish to be Gérard Depardieu. Casting him as Cyrano in the 1991 film was a stroke of genius, for Depardieu is one of a long line of French stars (Edith Piaf, Yves Montand *et les autres*) who have risen from the gutter to the glitter. The French love their heroes, real or fictional, to have had a past that is depraved, deprived or delinquent – an outsider who forces his or her way in.

They love Depardieu for what he does off-screen, for who he really is, a complete turnabout from the old Hollywood system where the screen image of the star was idolised. Depardieu is a man first, a film star second – the man who turned down a film role because the harvest was due in his vineyard; the man who says had he been a woman he would have made love with director Ridley Scott; the man who is called 'a force of nature'.

Faddishness

The French are the most faddish people in the world; They love ideas, concepts, innovations – playing around with things, like democracy, railway systems, architecture. It's not the practical end of the road they're interested in, but the journey, the possibilities, hence the way they drive, as though safe arrival at their destina-

> 66 The French love their heroes and heroines, real or fictional, to have had a past that is depraved, deprived or delinquent. 99

tion was the last thing on their minds. They will take anything if it's fashionable. They love the latest clothes, the latest slang, the latest films, the latest gadgets, but 'latest' lasts only a few days and then it's on to the newest latest. Not for nothing is *passé* a French concept.

At a railway in south-west France, a machine that

dug the ballast under the track looked as though it had been designed by Dr. Seuss for *The Cat in the Hat*, as it inched forward, with rods shooting out of the sides, swivelling down, thrashing about, grinding into the stone. The four men operating the monster were clearly delighted with it – for it was state-of-the-art-*moderne*.

What matters is being up-to-date. People will happily accept the hard sell if they think the paint on the item is still wet. They do not share the British cynicism about advertising. The British admire the advertisement but don't buy the product, whereas the French don't value the advertisement as an art form in itself, but throw themselves headlong at the product. They love to feel that life is fast moving, energetic and stylish.

> **66 What matters is being up-to-date. The French will happily accept the hard sell if they think the paint on the item is still wet. 99**

At one extreme this results in an elitist technocracy; at the other in obnoxious – but usually short-lived – cults, such as that of the '*Dûr-Etre*' baby ('It's hard to be a baby'), where hordes of teenage girls mimicked the words of a pop song of that name and wandered about with babies' dummies dangling on ribbons around their necks.

In this, as in everything they do, the French seesaw constantly from the superb to the absurd.

Farmers at heart

Intellectually and spiritually, the average French citizen still identifies very much with the land, romanticising rural and village life to a wholly improbable degree. Inside every Bordeaux technocrat, Parisian restauranteur or Grenoble academic still beats the heart of a genuine *paysan*.

To these displaced urban French, the burly farmer – gunning down the local squirrels, fattening fettered geese for their foie gras and counting

> 66 Intellectually and spiritually, the average French citizen still identifies very much with the land, romanticising rural and village life to a wholly improbable degree. 99

every corn of cob in their fields – can be forgiven because of all he does to protect a way of life that they abandoned long ago. Even as the sophisticates fume at the wheels of their Peugeots and Renaults, in traffic jams caused by agricultural industrial action (the throwing up of barricades of old tractors, rioting, lobbing stones at the police), they feel deep empathy and spiritual communion with the culprits, among whom could well be their grandfathers.

Fifty-nine million philosophers

From this rural base, the French have stormed the intellectual high ground. The Americans, British, Germans, Koreans, Chinese and others fight to take the lead in the seedy business of making money. The French are more concerned to protect and promote European culture, and by this they mean de Maupassant, Degas, Debussy – the only culture worth having, as far as they are concerned. The French only acknowledge other nations' culture as adjuncts to their own.

> **It is the passion for matters of the intellect that makes the French natural philosphers. They worship ideas and those who generate them.**

It is the passion for matters of the intellect that makes them natural philosphers. They are a people that eat, drink and breathe philosophy. There is not a farmer, fisherman, waiter, car-worker, shop assistant or housewife who isn't a closet Descartes or Diderot, a Saint-Simon or Sartre. The reason for this is that the French are brain-driven. They worship ideas and those who generate them, even if the ideas are only in vogue for the briefest periods.

Sartre's existentialism, born in the Occupation and flourishing in the late 1940s and '50s, was a spent force by the 1960s – but it doesn't matter: new ideas are like buses on the Paris autobus system, there will always be another along in a few minutes.

This preoccupation with perceptions and conceptions makes the French much harder to govern than the Germans, who have a natural tendency towards acceptance of authority, or the English, who will grumble but do as they're told. The French examine every facet of modern life through a philosophical microscope. In the whole Western world there exists the problem of unemployment. To the Americans, Spanish, Dutch, Danes, Italians, British, Germans and Belgians it is exactly that – a problem of unemployment. To the French it is 'a question of civilisation'.

They have an expression: *le discours*. It can mean anything from idle chatter to a formal speech, but their favoured use of it is as 'a piece of discursive reasoning'. Those skilled in this craft (which is about 95% of the population), are held in high esteem. A French man or woman will hold up a piece of nifty reasoning with the same pride that another might feel when displaying an Impressionist painting, a Fabergé egg or a Sèvres vase.

And so, in Cafés Philo across France, argument rages on every subject from literature to liberty, from privilege to privacy. Away with old thoughts, let us embrace the new. At their computers from Cannes to Calais, from Nantes to Nancy, budding philosophers are tapping away, formulating new theories, new conceits. All over France, 59 million philosophers are hungrily waiting.

> **❝ A French man or woman will hold up a piece of nifty reasoning with the same pride that another might feel when displaying an Impressionist painting, a Fabergé egg or a Sèvres vase. ❞**

Attitudes & Values

Despite a past littered with revolutions and upheavals, the French have maintained a stable and unchanging outlook on what matters in life. They have a high regard for the intellect, for qualifications and for the products of certain academic institutions. For, although there are remnants of the old class system among the French (a few aristocrats whose forebears were not pruned by Madame la Guillotine), France is above all else a meritocracy.

> **Although there are remnants of the old class system among the French, France is above all else a meritocracy.**

In the United States the belief is that anyone can do anything if they really want to. In Britain the belief is anyone can do anything if they prove they are able to. In France the belief is that anyone can do anything they are qualified to do, and must be allowed to do so unchallenged once they have proved that they went through the right channels, observed the right formalities.

This gives French politicians carte blanche to come up with bold, imaginative, costly and silly projects that receive widespread approval even when they become disastrous failures, simply because they were originally so bold, imaginative, etc. Despite Chernobyl, the French proceeded apace with their nuclear programme. Concorde was a financial disaster, but a conceptual triumph. In the 1980s they began excitedly prospecting for oil beneath Paris. One has to admire such wild and terrifying aspirations. The French have the courage to experiment, fail, and then experiment again – not a nation burdened by its past, but one that revels in its ability to use the present as a springboard into the future.

A passion for roots

France enjoys a huge amount of land relative to the size of her population. That is why the British, Dutch, Belgian, German and Japanese visitors experience a feeling of space on arrival in France. There seems to be plenty of room for everyone. But the French don't see it that way. They feel there is not enough land to go round. Not only is there an undercurrent of resentment that immigrants are taking up houses, flats and jobs, there is festering resentment about the possession of every ditch, manure heap or nettle patch in the entire country.

> **The French have the courage to experiment, fail, and then experiment again.**

Land – the ownership thereof – is the one bone of contention which can shatter family loyalties and general bonhomie. *Jean de Florette* and *Manon des Sources* were no figments of Pagnol's imagination.

Gérard Depardieu blew himself up in the former and Daniel Auteuil hanged himself in the latter because of a feud about the ownership of land. Every French citizen would understand and empathise with the characters in both films. There may well be enough land to go round, theoretically. In practice there can never be enough, not if the population were to be halved or quartered. From Balzac to Zola, French literature teaches that, without the slightest compunction, a French farmer will kill his brother, uncle, aunt, niece and nephew for a clod or two of soil. He will coax the deeds to the land from his own grandmother and then lock her up for life in a smelly outhouse if it means he gets sufficient earth to plant just one more row of beans. Of course, even French literature is mere art, but French art has a habit of imitating life.

> **66 From Balzac to Zola, French literature teaches that a French farmer will kill his brother, uncle, aunt, niece and nephew for a clod or two of soil. 99**

It doesn't matter where the land is – it may be the lush meadows of Normandy, the rolling hills of the Cévennes, the sandy dunes of Les Landes, or the harsh stony terraces of Herault – there can never be enough of it. Most French peasant farmers work land that has been in their family for generations, land that their ancestors hacked at and drenched with the sweat of their bodies back in the days of the *ancien régime* when they were little better than serfs. The one lasting achievement of the French Revolution, in their eyes, was that it gave the land to the people, and no scheming cousin from over the hill is going to take it away.

The exception is, of course, the sale of unwanted plots of land to the perfidious English with their crazy desires to buy every ruined barn and pigsty from Roscoff to Rocamadour. It's one thing to be cheated out of a pebble or two by a blood relative; it's quite another thing to fleece a total stranger, and a foreign one at that.

Class and the bourgeoisie

The French are aware of their position in society's pecking order at all times. Since they invented the bourgeoisie, it's only right that they should provide the most and best examples. Bourgeois is not so much a status as a way of life; one that manages at one and the same time to

> **Since they invented the bourgeoisie, it's only right that they should provide the most and best examples.**

delight and disgust them. What they like about being bourgeois is the security, the lack of vulgarity, the reliability, the continuity of life. What they detest is the predictability, the lack of curiosity, the respectability. It is an inner conflict that they have so far been unable to resolve.

17

It is also a state of mind, and it is this that divides France into its class system. On the surface, all is bold and growing equality, *egalité*. French waiters and their clients no longer call each other 'Sir', but beneath the surface old divisions remain. There are few working-class lawyers, professors, doctors or accountants. It is still extremely difficult for the son of a car worker to become an architect, and even harder for his daughter.

Even the bourgeoisie are divided into different classes:

The *grande* bourgeoisie come from what other countries would call 'good families', with known names – de Gaulle was a typical example. They played a great part in France's great past.

The *bonne* bourgeoisie are scions of a younger breed, far more likely to play a great part in France's great future.

The *petite* bourgeoisie are dismissed with the greatest contempt because they haven't played a great part in France's great past and they probably won't be allowed to play a great part in France's great future.

What the French do about this ambiguous state of affairs is what they do best, they ignore it, not so much in the hope that it will go away, but in the expectation that it will not matter. The French nobility, what's left of it, has long been ignored. It hasn't gone away. It still holds regular cocktail parties, banquets and balls that are both lavish and secretive, but nobody takes any notice. It even holds fox hunts, but the French do not bestir themselves to sabotage such actions. Better to ignore than oppose.

It is difficult to distinguish one bourgeois from another: the *grande* bourgeoisie are impeccably dressed at all times and don't speak to anyone outside their own class; the *bonne* bourgeoisie are impeccably dressed and speak to everyone; the *petite* bourgeoisie are impeccably dressed and speak only to complain, so it is better not to call anyone French 'bourgeois'. The *grande* bourgeoisie know they're *grande* bourgeoisie and won't thank you for stating the obvious. The *bonne* bourgeoisie will worry that they are being lumped with the *petite* bourgeoisie and will be insulted. It's best to ignore the entire notion.

> **66 As it is difficult to distinguish one bourgeois from another it's best to ignore the entire notion. 99**

Snobbery

The French are great snobs. They are snobbish about the dogs they own, clinging to breeds that have long passed out of fashion elsewhere (such as cocker spaniels and 'Scotties'). They are snobbish about where they live (there are *arrondissements* in Paris where a mere broom cupboard costs millions of euros); they are snobbish about what they wear. They are also very snobbish about schools. There are a number of prestigious schools in France that lead on to the higher echelons of society. A child who goes to the 'right' *lycée* in Paris may proceed to the National Administration School or the Polytechnic School and thence to the upper strata of the civil service (known as Grand Corps d'Etat – the sort of title that would be unthinkable elsewhere). Most high-level politicians have graduated from these institutions. There are those who graduated from all three and joined a very powerful old-boy network.

66 What makes French snobbery easier to accept is that it is based on good taste. 99

They are snobbish about where they shop, eat, play tennis, take dancing lessons, holiday, and go to church (the 10% that do attend Mass). What makes French snobbery a little easier to accept is that it is based on good taste.

Feminism and femininity

French women still look as though they expect doors to be opened for them, cases to be carried, seats to be vacated. They present themselves as elegant creatures who need men in the way that a perfect jewel needs the proper setting. It is still perfectly acceptable to compliment a French woman in a way that would rile her English or American sisters.

It is logical, reasonable and sensible to demand equal pay, equal access to the top jobs, equal opportunities in work and education. But they have not the slightest wish to surrender the power that they have traditionally wielded so subtly, whether as good wives or good mistresses.

> **❝ French women believe in feminism, but not at the price of femininity. They still want to be wooed and seduced. ❞**

French women believe in feminism, but not at the price of femininity. They still want to be wooed and seduced. The idea of hating men or wishing to exist without them seems ridiculous to the vast majority of French women. What is the point of flaunting fashion or flair if men aren't around to admire them? Where is the fun or frisson in life if men aren't around to play their part?

This approach is perfectly acceptable to most French men, who are as excited by women's brains as they are by women's bodies. Madame de Pompadour and Madame de Maintenon might not have been pin-ups, but they knew how to run the country better than their royal lovers. The ideal combination for a Frenchman is not 'a healthy mind in a healthy body', but 'a sexy mind in a sexy body'.

Wealth

The moneyed French keep a much lower profile than their Italian, German, or American counterparts. They wear dark suits, drive dark cars, live in dark houses, drink dark wine and meet in dark corners.

On the few occasions when they emerge into the light of day, they do not trot along to Carrefour or Intermarché. They do not frequent public transport. They (and the farmers) are the only French people who do not spend their holidays in campsites; there are still vast, dark villas in totally untrendy resorts where all is tranquillity and gracious living.

Let others flaunt their riches in vulgar displays of jewellery, fast cars and fat cigars, the wealthy French will have none of that. They live quietly in elegant houses in discreet districts, surrounded by high creeper-covered walls and protected by *chiens méchants* (the French are very honest when it comes to labelling vicious dogs – where others describe such beasts as 'guard dogs', the French are willing to admit openly that these animals are 'spiteful', 'nasty', 'wicked').

> **The moneyed French wear dark suits, drive dark cars, live in dark houses, drink dark wine and meet in dark corners.**

This modest approach to affluence is a far cry from the ostentation of the aristos of old. Gone are the châteaux, the parks, the glittering balls and the annual horse-whipping of the peasants. Since they are almost never to be seen in public, their superiority has to be administered quickly and subtly on the few occasions when they come across the bourgeois or the Bolshevik. They do not sneer at those who cannot afford the very best, they simply affect not to understand them.

Get into a conversation with two very wealthy French men or women (it's difficult, but it can be done if there's a run on taxis on a wet day in

> **66 The wealthy do not sneer at those who cannot afford the very best, they simply affect not to understand them. 99**

the Rue de Rivoli) and within seconds they will turn to each other, as if to say: "It is not possible for me to understand what is being said here. Is it possible for you to understand what is being said here?" The effect is withering.

There are, of course, a few select occasions and venues where wealth is more openly on display: at the Prix de l'Arc de Triomphe, at the Paris Opéra, and at any display of imported Christmas cakes with famous labels. In general, however, to make contact with the French well-to-do, you need a number of things: an immense amount of patience, considerable histrionic ability (to pretend you are something that you are not), impeccable manners, excellent French, a torch (to light up those dark corners where the wealthy are to be found), and some poisoned meat (for the *chiens méchants*).

Religion

Despite their Catholic tradition, the French have always been religious mavericks. For a century or more they had their own Pope in Avignon rivalling and fighting the Pope in Rome.

Catholicism has suited them, with its emphasis on sin and exoneration rather than guilt and shame. The notion that it is all right to sin so long as you repent afterwards fits in well with the French insistence that there must be a way round every problem.

> **66 The notion that it is all right to sin so long as you repent afterwards fits in well with the French insistence that there must be a way round every problem. 99**

Churches in France are heavy, dark, depressing buildings, smelling of aniseed and carbolic, presided over by priests who have lost much of the authority they used to have within the community, and who are anyway much more concerned with the collapse of Socialism than they are by the decline in Catholicism.

What the French have very cunningly done, is to abandon many of the duties and burdens of religion, but keep the feast days and holidays. This is why so many foreigners are to be seen, on the Day of the Assumption of the Blessed Virgin Mary, wandering despondently through the streets of towns where their favourite restaurants are shut. It is yet another example of the French plucking the good things from life, abandoning the rest, and having no conscience at all about what happens in consequence.

French cars

There is little value in a second-hand French car. This is why there are no second-hand car salesmen to be found in Reims, Lyons or Marseilles.

When the French buy a new car, they buy it for life – which means about three years in the case of the car and rather less in the case of too many drivers. French roads are littered with slaughter, even though they have always favoured small, rather timid-looking cars. They do so partly because such cars are brave – ascending any sort of gradient is a major battle against great odds – and partly because small cars are cheaper to tax than big cars (cars are taxed according to their horsepower). There are, therefore, very few luxury French limousines.

Although not made any more, the darling of all French cars is still the 2CV, which would look more at home on the end of a pole on a fairground carousel, but which is economical, surprisingly comfortable (except when it brakes or goes round a corner), amazingly reparable, and which (significantly) the French call 'the world's most intelligent car'. This is the sort of

> **“ The darling of all French cars is still the 2CV, which would look more at home on the end of a pole on a fairground carousel. ”**

phrase that would take an advertising copywriter an entire lifetime to dream up, but it comes naturally to the French because they look for intelligence in everything that moves.

Behaviour

The French are a formal people, rigid in their thinking and much of their behaviour. From Napoleon's time onwards they have always loved codes, the stricter the better: of etiquette, fashion, ethics, diplomacy, art, literature and law.

They believe intensely in what they call *la règle*: everything that matters should be done in the right way and in the right place and at the right time. What they don't like, and ignore at their discretion, are petty regulations – about parking, smoking, driving, hygiene, and where you may and may not urinate.

To the French, there is a world of difference between rules and formalities. The former are to be ignored, the latter strictly observed. This is exemplified by the elaborate way they sign off their letters. Where the Americans and English are happy to scrawl 'best wishes', 'all the best', or (at the latter's most formal) 'yours faithfully', the French insist on *'Nous vous prions d'agréer, Monsieur, l'assurance de nos sentiments respectueux*' (We beg you to believe in the assurance of our respectful sentiments), and (at their most informal) '*N'oublie pas de nous donner de tes nouvelles de temps en temps, s'il te plaît*' (Don't forget to give us news of yourself from time to time, please).

Language is seen as embodying dignity, so language has been formalised for its own protection. French dictionaries even contain pages of phrases to be used as 'The Mechanics of Argument'.

Being stylised is as important as having style.

Standards

At heart, the French are traditionalists. Although they dearly love revolutions, pulling everything down and starting from scratch (offering endless scope for debate and discussion), they disapprove of shifts in behaviour. Everything must be done *comme il faut* (properly), an expression that applies equally to getting married and getting

> **Everything must be done *comme il faut* (properly), an expression that applies equally to getting married and getting drunk, stuffing a duck or filling in a form.**

drunk, stuffing a duck and filling in a form, addressing an envelope and addressing a teacher. There is an established order of things, and the order was established by the French.

The desire to maintain standards is best seen on any

holiday in the summer. Where the Spanish, the
Italians, the British, and even the Germans, relax sufficiently to let a little stubble grow, or mealtimes
become irregular, or their dress become bizarre and ill
co-ordinated, the French behave as though they were
still under the microscope of
real life.

> **66 Even on holiday the
> French behave as though
> they were still under the
> microscope of real life. 99**

French men and women
take two hours over their
morning toilette. Watch any
Frenchman at a campsite in the summer and see how
long he spends shaving, trimming his moustache, and
on general ablutions. By the time he has finished, it is
the hour of the apéritif.

Wives cook three-course luncheons which they
serve to their husbands in the sweltering heat at little
tables with linen napkins and polished cutlery. The
white wine stands in an ice bucket in what little shade
there is; the red wine is *chambré*-ed in the tent.
Everything is correct – the bread, the cheese, the
salad, the sauce.

Monsieur eats greedily. Madame stands behind
him, and a little to the side, nodding happily. She will
do the washing-up immediately the meal is finished.
All will be neat and tidy before any other activity is
even considered. Meanwhile, all over the rest of the
campsite, foreigners are dropping food out of their
hands, their mouths, their pockets.

The family

The French are very attached to the family – blood is definitely thicker than (mineral) water. They take pride in their children, partly because for many years France suffered a declining birth-rate – indeed, their defeat in the Second World War has been attributed (by them) to the simple fact that the Germans bred more successfully than they did in the first couple of decades of the 20th century. There are still tax incentives available in France to encourage and reward having a large family.

The elderly are given respect, the young are given affection. There is an interdependence in French families, where grandparents, aunts and uncles may well live very near the immediate family. All generations are included in family plans, holidays, discussions, meals and celebrations.

Children are encouraged to air their thoughts at a tender age, so that they are often good conversationalists by the time they are seven or eight years old. One of the delights of French life is the spectacle of an entire family of three or four generations all enjoying themselves at the same restaurant, or at a party. And one of the most severe sanctions that can be imposed on a child by a parent is to be banned from such a function. One

❝One of the delights of French life is the spectacle of an entire family of three or four generations enjoying themselves at a restaurant or party.❞

French family, whose son committed some mild breach of family etiquette, ceremoniously removed his place-setting at the table for dinner that evening, frighteningly reminiscent of poor Dreyfus* being marched round the parade ground, having the buttons torn from his uniform and his sword snapped in half. But the son uncomplainingly did as he was told and ate alone in the kitchen.

Children

English children look like devils and behave like devils. French children look like angels and behave like devils. Watch any group of beautifully groomed and attired French tots on the beach or in the park, and, the moment all grown-up backs are turned, see the mud or sand stuffed into eyes and ears, hear the thud of spade or boot on knee, thrill to the fusillade of stones or gravel as one little angel pelts another. This is because anarchy sets in when French children are let off the lead. They are at their bourgeois best

> **66** English children look like devils and behave like devils. French children look like angels and behave like devils. **99**

---

*Captain Dreyfus, whose wrongful conviction and deportation to Devil's Island in 1894 (for supposedly revealing military secrets to Germany), outraged and divided French opinion.

hand-in-hand with an adult (mama, papa, grandmère, au pair, nanny) in formal, structured settings: a fête, a family celebration, an outing. The sight of a crocodile of 30 or 40 French children, marching hand-in-hand in pairs, is as enchanting as it is still commonplace.

On being introduced to an adult, they shake hands solemnly, or offer their cheek to be kissed with becoming modesty and not a trace of embarrassment.

> **Every beach has its swimming school. The training is rigorous but the children are seldom allowed into the water.**

The French go to great lengths to make special provision for their children, especially at holiday time. Every beach in France has its swimming school, presided over by elderly swimming instructors who are even thinner than French cyclists. The training is rigorous and comprehensive, but the children are seldom allowed into the water.

Next door is a supervised sports area where the little 'ducks' and 'dolphins' are taught how to climb ropes, turn somersaults and crawl through lengths of pipe by bronzed teenagers who take their responsibilities very seriously.

Because a hundred years ago there weren't enough French children, this has led to generations of youngsters being loved and valued to the point of being spoilt. French children, therefore, have grown up sensing that they are most important. They have evidence of this in the grooming they receive, in the way they are included in adult conversation, in the effusive admiration that aunts and uncles, grandparents and godparents bestow upon them. They love the way they are worshipped. It's just that when the worshippers aren't looking...

Elders

The traditional ways of keeping a family together are still prevalent in much of France – in rural areas especially. The idea of sending Granny into a *'Tiers Temps'* (Third Age) residential home is anathema to the French, who see it as natural to look after one's own. Besides it is so much cheaper, one always has a babysitter en suite, and, crucially, one can keep an eye on one's heritage.

Animals

The rural French remain primitive hunters, slaughtering anything from larks to wild boar. To them, there are only two reasons for the existence of animals – because they taste good, or because they are useful (as sheepdogs, guard dogs, laboratory mice, etc.). The notion of 'endangered species' doesn't exist because there is only one species worth protecting – their own.

The urban French used to share these views, owning only utilitarian or display pets – an Alsatian to protect your property, or a poodle to show off your exquisite taste in *à la mode* accessories – but they are becoming increasingly pet conscious. There are some 10 million dogs in France, many of whom eat at table with their owners, and an alarming number of whom accompany their owners on motor bikes.

By and large the French have none of the nauseous sentimentality the English have for animals. It would never occur to the French to have such an institution for homeless animals as the Battersea Dogs Home – for who would want to adopt a dog whose owners had abandoned it in the first place? Pet dogs who trespass on to other people's land run the risk of being surreptitiously poisoned. In France, stray dogs are either adopted by an entire community or destroyed – depending on which is quicker.

> 66 What the French are best at is tasks that are totally self-absorbing – cooking, anything to do with the arts, individual sport. 99

Driving

What the French are best at is tasks that are totally self-absorbing – cooking, anything to do with the arts, individual sport. What they are hopeless at is any occupation that requires giving consideration to others, like team games, living in close proximity on a crowded campsite, or parking. This is why they rely so heavily on a highly structured system of social etiquette: without it they would be at each other's throats.

Their self-centredness is most apparent in the way they drive. Anarchy holds the steering wheel, and the real French character emerges. Traffic rules are regarded by the French as interesting suggestions which might be considered if one hadn't something far more important in mind.

> **66 Traffic rules are regarded by the French as interesting suggestions which might be considered if one hadn't something far more important in mind. 99**

The average French man (and woman) sits patriotically at the wheel of a Peugeot, Citroën or Renault, switches on the engine, shoves the car into gear and then drives the length and breadth of Europe as though it were a private estate. They are not just bad drivers, they are insanely dangerous drivers. Every major road interchange is like a crowded dance floor, with cars waltzing up to each other, bumping, jostling for space, everybody knowing where they want to go and madly resenting the presence of those in the way.

One of the most exciting things to do in France is to try to use a pedestrian crossing. Those who are slow, through age or indisposition, should resign themselves to living out their days on one side of the street. One of the first laws the German army imposed on the citizens of Paris in 1940 was that they should cross the roads only at specifically appointed places. The Third Reich was, from that moment, doomed.

> **They have a faith in a car's braking system that puts Joan of Arc's faith in God to shame.**

The French don't believe they are the world's worst drivers, although the carnage on French roads suggests otherwise. They drive facing sideways, backwards, upwards (if their car has a sun roof), with perverse individuality and scorn for impending disaster. They ignore worsening road conditions with a shrug of the shoulders and a flick of the Gauloise. They have a faith in the average car's braking system that puts Joan of Arc's faith in God to shame. They regard every stop sign, every crossroad, every roundabout as an affront to their individual liberty. 'Prudence' say the Warning signs at the side of French autoroutes. It's not even up for negotiation.

Manners

Butting in on each other's conversations is not considered rudeness by the French, but proof that they find the exchange interesting and wish to take part. What passes for the stock opening conversational gambits among other peoples ("What do you do for a living?",

"How much do you make?", "Are you married?", and "Do you have any children?") are regarded as none of your business – '*Occupe-toi de tes oignons*' (Mind your own onions), as they say. Better instead to talk about art, culture, or best of all, politics. Everyone in France has views on these subjects – even the plumber who comes to mend a burst pipe will be happy to rest his wrench to discuss Voltaire.

Gestures

The French invented body language. To watch a *gendarme* on traffic control is to witness an elaborate modern ballet – the twirling baton, the palm of the hand thrust forward to bring hundreds of vehicles to a halt, the abrupt inclination of the head that allows them to proceed, the raising of the judgemental eyebrow if all is not in order.

66 In conversation, French hands are never still. They display the state of the mind, heart and soul of the parties involved. 99

In conversation, French hands are never still. They give shape, form and size to ideas. They display the state of the mind, heart and soul of the parties involved. Where others use the inflection of the voice to show how they feel, the French use eyes, hands, lips and shoulders to reveal a full range of emotions. They kiss the tips of their fingers to show they approve strongly of something or somebody. They pull the hand across the forehead when they are fed up. They raise their shoulders when confronted by the ridiculous. They stroke their cheeks with the back of the hand as a sign that they are bored. They purse their lips and exhale when they are exas-

> **66 With subliminal awareness of their deep internal anarchy, the French rigidly respect officialdom but hate officials. 99**

perated. They have gestures for disapproval, incredulity, superiority, apology, amazement, surprise, bewilderment and frustration. Which is why it is considered grossly impolite to talk with one's hands in one's pockets.

Respect and insults

With subliminal awareness of their deep internal anarchy, the French rigidly respect officialdom but hate officials. Thus the President of France must be accorded full honours, rituals, escorts of motorbikes, and so on, but it is not necessary to value him as a person. The French flag is much respected: in some French black and white films of the 1930s and late '40s it was hand-coloured on the film stock itself, so that it stood out incongruously from everything else. The French national anthem also commands respect, perhaps because a lot of it is an encouragement to direct action.

But respect in France has to be earned. There is none of the putting-a-polite-face-on-things that is to be found among other peoples. The French, especially Parisians, are phenomenally rude when they wish to be. There is none of the unthinking or forgetful rudeness of other nations. When the French are rude it is because they consider that the occasion demands it.

In particular, the French are happy to be rude to complete strangers. If you ring a wrong number in France, you can expect an earful of quite outrageous insults. Among friends, insults are also frequently traded, but with no permanent damage to relationships. In other countries, if you insult someone, you do it for life. In France, people insult each other dreadfully one day, and act as though nothing had been said the next.

> **66 When the French are rude it is because they consider that the occasion demands it. 99**

The French are very good at insults, seen at their best in city rush-hour confrontation. They have a rich language for expletives and a lively imagination. Without knowing a word of French, it is possible to know that you have been insulted, for the French present their insults dramatically, making full use of the grimace and the ugly gesture.

They have dozens of words for the unmentionable, but tend to concentrate on only one or two. '*Connard*' and '*con*' are routine insults (the latter once held to be extremely vulgar but now used routinely in conversation). The more prudish may not use the word as such, but spell it out '*c...o...n*'. It can be translated acceptably as 'bloody fool'.

Etiquette

The French are, *par excellence*, a sociable people, but they value their privacy. They jealously guard their moments of meditation, their daily family discussions or their right to sit alone in a bar peering into a glass of Pernod. So if they see someone they know sitting outside a café, they will acknowledge only if acknowledged, and approach only if the person indicates that their company is welcome.

> **66 The French parliament once debated the question as to whether a gentleman in a *pissoir*, recognising a female passer-by, should lift his hat to her. 99**

They observe a strict code of etiquette and are adamant that certain things are not done in public. Men do not comb their hair in the street, neither do women apply their make-up. No matter how hot the day, clothes are not discarded as one promenades along the street. The French parliament once debated at length the question as to whether a gentleman in a *pissoir*, when recognising a female passer-by, should lift his hat to her.

On the Métro and on French buses seats are reserved for the disabled and pregnant women.

Should some gum-chewing layabout sit in one of these seats, he will soon be asked to move by one better entitled to it, who will have the manifested moral support of all the other passengers.

They respect the space of others by respecting their own space and carefully monitoring what they do within it, not in case someone is watching, but because they assume everyone is bound to be watching. So, whereas drivers caught in an English traffic jam resort to picking their noses as a way of passing the time, drivers caught in a French traffic jam scrutinise themselves in the driving mirror, and make minor but important adjustments to their ties, hair, eyebrows or moustaches. The distinction is a question of style.

> **66 Frenchmen pee everywhere. They pee while they smoke, talk, fish, garden, adjust carburettors, mix cement or walk horses. 99**

The one exception to all this is the Emptying of the Male Bladder. Frenchmen pee everywhere – by the side of the road (towards the traffic as well as away from it): into rivers, lakes and canals; against trees, shrubs and lamp-posts; behind shops, garages, railway stations. They pee while they smoke, talk, fish, garden, adjust carburettors, mix cement or walk horses.

A visitor was holidaying in France, by the sea. It was midnight. He had eaten well at the village restaurant, and drunk just enough wine to reach that point where life is infinitely good. The sea was calm, the moon was full. He was as near Paradise as he expects to be this side of the grave. And then three Frenchmen lurched out of the night and peed in the ocean. The reverie died instantly. But what really upset him was the cordial way all three wished him "*Bonne nuit*" as they zipped up their trousers and left.

Greetings

Foreigners often fail to appreciate the formal code of greeting in France. The French shake hands with everyone (family, children, strangers), at home, on the way to work, at work, on leaving work, on the way home from work, etc. Thus, in an office that employs perhaps a dozen people, no work will be done for the first half hour while those who have not met since the day before, remind each other who they are.

> 66 It is regarded as extremely bad manners to shake hands with someone twice in a day, as though one had not taken adequate notice the first time. 99

However, it is important to remember with whom one has shaken hands on any one day. The French regard it as extremely bad manners to shake hands twice, as though one had not taken adequate notice the first time.

It is still the custom to say "*Bonjour*" and "*Au revoir*" to one and all when entering or leaving a shop or bar. This is not because the French are excessively polite. It is because they see acknowledging the existence of others as a way of avoiding being rude. The distinction may seem unbearably subtle to others, but to the French it is most important. Manners maketh civilisation to them. Without rigid formalities, the primitive in them would assuredly assert itself.

> **The French greeting kiss, as distinct from the French Kiss, is a subtle affair.**

This is why the structure is so carefully graded. There are those shopkeepers to whom one should say "*Bonjour, monsieur*", and those to whom one should say "*Bonjour, monsieur. Ça va?*", and those to whom one should say "*Bonjour, monsieur. Ça va?...*" and a whole lot more.

Learning the French language is child's play compared with learning the Etiquette of Kissing. The French greeting kiss, as distinct from the French Kiss, is a subtle affair. In eastern France, it's two kisses – left then right. In western France, it's two kisses, right then left. In Paris, it's four kisses – left, right, left, right, in south west France, three. Woe betide the floundering foreigner who moves right where he should have moved left. As a general rule, observe what's going on around you and act accordingly – 'when in the Rhône, do as the Rhôneans do'.

The insistent formality of French greetings makes huge inroads into their lives. On a beach near Biarritz, eight Parisians lay down on their smart beach towels to sunbathe. Along came a ninth. All eight stood up, to shake hands with or embrace the ninth. All nine lay down. Along came a tenth. All nine stood up, to shake hands with or embrace the tenth. This went on until there were 23 people in the group. Very little was accomplished in the way of sunbathing.

Tu-ing and *vous*-ing

One of the few things most people learn about the French is that they have two words for 'you' – *tu* and *vous*. What nobody ever learns is when to use which.

It is perfectly polite to use '*tu*' to a dog, even if you have never met him (or her) before. But it is safest not to use '*tu*' to a human being until he or she does it to you first, for to be '*tutoi*-ed' is to be admitted into the inner sanctum of French life, to be accepted, to be granted the privileged status of close friend.

> **To be *'tutoi-ed'* is to be admitted into the inner sanctum of French life, to be granted the status of close friend.**

'*Tu*' is not merely a grammatical form. It is an important but subtle social signal. There are some you will never say '*tu*' to, not if the Foreign Legion were to take up knitting or the local bakery were to start producing sliced white bread. There are some French couples who never use '*tu*' to one another in their entire married lives.

Leisure & Pleasure

Annual holidays

The French are great holiday-makers for they have discovered one great truth – that it is possible to get away from it all and yet take it all with you.

Long ago most French people abandoned the expensive hotels in the expensive resorts and took to '*le camping*' with a gusto that few others manage. All over southern Europe (the French seldom go north) their beautiful tents are to be seen: one section for living quarters, one section for sleeping quarters, one section for cooking quarters and one section as a garage and workshop.

The family takes its wine, its food, its bicycles, its recreation and, most important, its culture with it. They eat French, they drink French, they relax French and they exercise French.

> **66 The French have discovered one great truth – that it is possible to get away from it all and yet take it all with you. 99**

Every possible holiday location in France, including the stops on the autoroutes, has its *parcours sportif*, a two- or three-mile circuit strewn with exercise points. Most French under the age of 50 spend half their holiday puffing and panting their way round them, stopping every so often to drip sweat and pull a hamstring or two on the parallel bars, sit-up benches, climbing ropes and monkey runs which the local council has so kindly provided.

The heady mixture of sun, sand, sea and swooning exhaustion reaches its high saltwater mark in the Club Mediterranée – a package holiday concept that allows a baffling range of choices. Started in the 1950s by Gérard Blitz as a 'strange cocktail of *la vie de château et la vie de sauvage*' they offer culture, a sense of community, sport, good food and wine, and a great sense of civilised adventure. In exotic locations from Corfu to Tahiti, they give the French a chance to holiday with the French.

> 66 The Club Mediterranée was designed as a 'strange cocktail of *la vie de château et la vie de sauvage*'. 99

Other holidays

The French have a generous helping of days off. With luck, these fall on Tuesdays or Thursdays, which enables the French to take Monday or Friday off as well, and thereby create a long weekend – a practice known as *faire le pont* ('to make the bridge'), but it might just as well be known as *faire le* point.

Like the Scots, the French often spend more time, money and effort celebrating the New Year than Christmas. In their religious festivals, they adopt a position halfway between the Spanish and Italian fervour in sun-scorched town squares, and the semi-apologetic gatherings of the English on rain-swept village greens. They are mindful of the religious back-ground of such occasions, but what they most enjoy is the food and drink at the end of the day and the old songs sung at the long wooden tables.

In country districts they are aware of every saint's day in the calendar, and most French towns and vil-lages still traditionally cele-brate their local saint with parades, feasting and often a *kermesse* – a boozy church fête at which it is possible for an innocent visitor to win a duck 'sufficient at the table for eight persons', but still alarmingly alive.

> **66 A *kermesse* is a boozy fête at which you could win a duck 'sufficient at the table for eight persons', but still alarmingly alive. 99**

Best of all holidays is Bastille Day (14th July 1789 was the day that signalled the end of the French monarchy), when everyone comes out on to the streets and throws fire crackers at each other in affirmation of the individual against the State.

Le weekend

It was a long time before the French allowed them-selves a workless weekend but it is now another of their obsessions.

Though many still visit those members of the family

who live '*la vie paysanne*' an increasing the number of French couples have taken to plundering the fast-growing outlets devoted to DIY, home gadgetry and products for the garden. The choice here is whether your priority is to create

> **The French cram so much into *le weekend* it is often quite a relief to get back to work.**

your own Versailles, Louvres or Jardin Exotique de Monaco. Monsieur Bricolage (400 branches) has everything from complete bathrooms to home tapestry kits. Each one of Gifi's 250 stores is an Aladdin's cave of all that is plastic, and where else could you buy a plinth for only 12 euros. Trees, fountains, wildlife, and 100-kg sacks of parrot food are all available from Jardiland (100 branches). The French love them all. If you add sport, clubbing, dancing, and outings to the theatre or cinema, the French cram so much into *le weekend* it is often quite a relief to get back to work.

Le sport

Everything stops for the Tour de France, when the entire population lines the route, breathless for that split second when several hundred cyclists whizz past on their *vélos* in one highly coloured blur. It is the most popular sporting event in France because it's bright, it's fast, it's essentially French, and you can drink for a couple of weeks while watching it. Cycling is a mania in France. At all times of the year, men as thin as cycle spokes hurtle up and down mountains, overtaking anything slower than a Porsche, covering hundreds of kilometres a day and living off a diet of water and adrenaline. Cycling glorifies the individual in his battle against the landscape, the elements, the odds (lorries are so much bigger), and punctures.

> **66 Cycling glorifies the individual in his battle against the landscape, the elements and the odds. 99**

The only team games that interest the French are are *le rugby* and *le football*, basketball and, to a lesser extent, volleyball. They play all four in a thoroughly French way, with speed, *élan*, audacity, and a lot of noise.

Betting on the horses

The French love horses – they love gymkhanas, horse shows and foxhunting – and, most of all, they love horse races. Drive into any French town and there, maddeningly placed with all the other signs on the wrong side of a major crossroads so that you see it too late, will be a sign that says '*Hippodrome*', indicating a racecourse.

Every Sunday, with an almost religious fervour, the French flock to their local *bistrot*, to place their bets on the Pari Mutuel Urbain (PMU), the horse-racing wing the official state gambling department. Then they toast their future success with an aperitif and trot home to watch the day's racing on television. They don't even seem to mind that in the long run, the state is the only winner, taking 33% of all bets.

Sex

Though they may not be the most beautiful, the French are physically one of the best presented people in the world. They know how to dress, move, stand, smile, frown and even pout in an attractive way.

Because they use their hands, face and bodies to communicate far more than the Anglo-Saxon peoples, they are at ease with their bodies, and this, together with their unquestioning belief in themselves, gives them considerable sex appeal. The young Jeanne Moreau may not have been as beautiful as Grace

❝Jean Gabin was not as handsome as Cary Grant, but he had more sex appeal in the tilt of his hat than Grant had in his entire body.❞

Kelly, but she was much sexier. Jean Gabin was certainly not as handsome as Cary Grant, but he had more sex appeal in the tilt of his hat than Grant had in his entire body.

The French have a pleasantly guileless approach to sex. In the old days they believed it was necessary for a young couple to be chaperoned – not in case the couple made love, but because it was expected that they would do so. Sex has always been seen as part of life, not as an extra to the curriculum.

What distinguishes the French sexually from others is that there are still many unwritten rules regarding sex. If a man invites a girl to his apartment, she can rest assured that he will make a pass at her. To do anything less would be an insult (in the eyes of the man) to them both. On the other hand, although a Frenchman might well make a pass at the wife of a friend or colleague, he would never make a pass at the friend or colleague's daughter. The first is permissible, part of the wonderful nip and tuck of French life. The second is unthinkable, an abject betrayal of friendship, because the daughter is not in a position to make an informed decision. Seduction is an art form to be practised only among equals.

> **66** Seduction is an art form to be practised only among equals. **99**

Humour

From the early days of cinema, the French have admired physical humour and clowning. They worshipped their own Jacques Tati and virtually adopted Buster Keaton and Jerry Lewis. Even today, French humour relies as much on what you don't say as what you do say, and is rooted in self-deprecating observation, rather than in flights of whacky fantasy. They approach verbal humour from an oblique angle, with the same subtlety they bring to love-making, but with a bigger laugh at the end.

The set pieces of mime, made famous by Marcel Marceau, are still *de rigueur*. In pedestrian precincts across the country, young men and

> **66** They approach verbal humour with the same subtlety they bring to love-making, but with a bigger laugh at the end. **99**

women pretend to be erecting deck chairs, to be stuck in revolving doors, to be carrying huge panes of glass on a windy day. No-one has yet discovered why.

Culture

It is the honest opinion of every French man and woman that France has always led the world in matters cultural – painting, literature, sculpture, cinema, music, mime, theatre, ballet – and how to die at dawn in a duel.

They may well be right, for they have always known how to make the everyday look exceptional, artistic: walking down a street, sitting at a café, reading a book. Their homes might lack some of the splendour and enthusiasm of the English and Americans (inside and out), but they are happy to be judged by the books on their shelves, the pictures on their walls, the compact discs in their music centres.

People in France fight, plot and train to reveal the breadth of their intellect. At a time when he was President of France, Giscard d'Estaing took time off to take part in a literary programme on television to discuss the works of Guy de Maupassant. Although facing the usual half dozen political crises at the time, the President hastily brushed up on the subject and appeared, suave, calm and (most important) erudite. The result of his labour was not the collapse of the government, but an improvement in his own standing and a sellout of de Maupassant's books throughout the country.

> **" French culture is French glory. Clashes between intellectuals have all the excitement and dynamism of a boxing match. "**

French culture is French glory. In *les evénèments* – the near-revolution of 1968 – the first targets of the workers and students in Paris were the Odéon Theatre, the Opéra Comique and the Beaux Arts: to the French, to grab the cultural high ground is to be unassailable. Clashes between intellectuals in France have all the excitement and dynamism of a boxing match – but without the blood.

Cinema

Just as the French make an art form of everyday life, so they make everyday life into an art form.

Dozens of French films consist of little more than several people (bored, lonely, jealous, mad, bewildered – but mostly bored) sitting down to a lengthy and wordless meal. In the hands of any other film-makers such *œuvres* would be worthless, but somehow the French make masterpieces out of the mundane. A

> **❝Many French films consist simply of several bored people sitting down to a lengthy and wordless meal.❞**

French audience will watch such a film and then go to a restaurant to discuss it and relate it to their own lives. It is arguable that this has its own rationale.

The other major genres of the French cinema are comedies and *policiers*. The first are brightly lit and genuinely funny, for the French have a great clowning tradition. The second are darkly lit (or not lit at all) and genuinely thrilling.

The French have always taken their film industry seriously. In 1940 Vichy officials pronounced: "If we have lost the war it is because of *Quai des Brumes*," an archetypal French melodrama of the 1930s starring Jean Gabin and Michèle Morgan, about an army deserter who rescues a young girl from a gang of crooks, with the kind of unhappy ending that French audiences adore.

The French invented the notion of the film director as '*auteur*', as the person who stamps his image of the world on the film, and his image of the film on the world. They also raised consciousness of the cinema as an art to a much higher plane through the classic *Cahiers du Cinéma*, magazines with deeply intellectual articles that were hard to follow but provoked an enormous amount of discussion and debate.

Television and radio

The best thing on French television used to be de Gaulle's frequent pleas to his fellow citizens to calm down, go home and leave everything to him. No-one since has used the medium so well. Television today is only important because it shows the news (which means what is happening in France and/or what the French are doing elsewhere), sport (the Tour de France, the French rugby team, racing from Chantilly), and old French films. The Arte channel, a French-German collaboration, has good documentaries. For the rest, there is a rash of grim and cheap game shows. One shining light – a literary and arts chat show called *Bouillon de Culture* ran for 25 years and attracted millions of

> 66 The French invented the notion of the film director as '*auteur*', as the person who stamps his image of the world on the film, and his image of the film on the world. 99

54

viewers, but this ended in 2002. Nevertheless, the topics it raised are still debated. Ideas take a long time to die in France.

The problem with television is that it keeps people at home, where debate is limited in terms of participants. The older French would rather be in a bar (where most television sport is watched) or a restaurant or a friend's house, talking about it.

French radio provides pop stations and local stations and nostalgic stations and serious music stations, and sports and news stations, and gimmicky phone-in and phone-out stations, but nothing that produces the brand loyalty that exists, for example, for BBC's Radio 4 in Britain.

66 French radio is used mainly as a background when people are driving to and from work. 99

One of the few hugely popular radio programmes is one where the presenter phones members of the public in the hope of catching them in embarrassing situations. A form of radio voyeurism, it provides suitable subjects for discussion, since the French are obsessed with all aspects of human behaviour. Other than this, French radio is used mainly as a background when people are driving to and from work.

Music

When put on hold while calling a French telephone

number, the listener hears not Scott Joplin's *The Entertainer*, nor Vivaldi's *Four Seasons* played on a synthesiser, but real modern jazz.

The French have managed to hold on to their traditional music. Within only a few minutes of being in France it is possible to hear the strains of piano accordion, soprano saxophone, violin, guitar and drums – the classic French ensemble. The rest of the world may have been taken over by the sounds of the U.K. and U.S., but not France.

> 66 People still sing songs about a young man and a young woman in love, just as they did a hundred years ago. 99

People still sing songs about a young man and a young woman in the spring, in a park, in a *fiacre*, in love, just as they did a hundred years ago. All French singers have tremendous vibrato and every French song is as much a piece of drama as a piece of music.

Literature

The French glory in their long-winded literature and poetry. They especially admire Proust (novelist and manic depressive), Voltaire (humanitarian and jailbird), Verlaine (poet and debauchee), Molière (comic dramatist who was denied holy burial) and Flaubert (novelist and perfectionist, who spent hours or days on a single sentence, seeking the right word). They also admire Baudelaire, Racine, Hugo, Dumas (*père et fils*), Rabelais, Pagnol and almost anyone who wrote in the French language.

Readers of Proust discover painfully the idea that the mind is a mass of memories and that we live our lives as servants of these memories, however firmly locked away. In a scene in one book, the

> **66 It's very French, the idea of touch, smell, sound unlocking the past. The tragedy of Proust's *A La Recherche du Temps Perdu* is that it takes seven volumes to do this. 99**

hero is in a hotel room, dabbing his mouth with a towel. The crispness of the towel reminds him of his childhood and a similar towel. In another scene, his teaspoon slips and the sound of it resonating against the cup reminds him of a bell in his cottage garden.

All this is very French – the idea of touch, smell, sound unlocking the past and reviving 50-year-old memories. The tragedy of Proust's *A La Recherche du Temps Perdu* is that it takes seven volumes to do this, and nobody yet has found a satisfactory way of translating the first sentence of Volume I into English.

The French are also devotees of the *bande dessinée*, those wonderful comic strip books which tell the adventures of Astérix, Tintin, Lucky Luke and others, and which they have raised to an art form in its own right. Here for once they abandon their strict approach to their own tongue, and use humorous and colloquial phrases, as though taking the opportunity to indulge all the things they are not allowed to write elsewhere. Readers of the *Astérix* series discover painlessly the entrenched nationalism of the French, who adore these comic books because they affirm that France is the centre of the world.

Newspapers and *Paris Match*

The French have a great number of regional papers and several national daily papers – one for the extreme Right, one for the extreme Left, one for the Right of Centre, one for the Left of Centre, etc.

They believe newspapers should consist of text rather than pictures, information rather than advertisements, serious matters not frivolous affairs. Life must be well balanced, however. The

> **❝The French have raised comic strip books to an art form in their own right.❞**

French have always been the world's finest high-wire artistes, so they have the satirical weekly *Canard Enchaîné* which pokes fun at the establishment in the same way as America's *The Onion*, or Britain's *Private Eye*.

They also have *Paris Match*, more an institution than a magazine. The French love it because it confirms all that they wish to believe about themselves, that they are smart, beautiful, clever, artistic, always in the limelight.

They do not see it in any way as exposing the faults, flaws, mistakes or weaknesses of France. If a *Paris Match* poll reveals that 71% of its readers think the French are racist, few are shocked. It is not a question of whether this is a morally good or bad result – it is a French result, and that is what matters.

> **66** They love *Paris Match* because it confirms all that they wish to believe about themselves. **99**

Paris Match proves that the rest of the world trails after the French, picking up their leads in fashion, cinema, literature, politics, design, technology, transport, town planning and the use of garlic. That is why it has survived the onslaught of television news coverage, where others have folded.

To succeed in Britain, you have to be like the Germans. To succeed in Germany, you have to be like the Americans. To succeed in America, you have to be like the Japanese. To succeed in France, you have to be like the French. *Paris Match* is exactly like the French.

Eating & Drinking

For the French, enjoyment of food in a good restaurant or in the home of a fine cook, is a spiritual experience, a neo-religious ritual. Indeed, the French find comfort, pride and solace in their food, as well as excitement and stimulation.

There are still many parts of France where two hours is allowed for lunch, though more and more people are opting for a shorter lunch-break and an earlier end to work, so they can get home to their families. They may then go out again, *en famille*, to eat their evening meal, for even a humble roadside café can offer a *blanquette de veau* every bit as good as in a top-class restaurant, at a fraction of the price.

> **❝ There is a little shop in St. Emilion that sells macaroons made to the same recipe since 1620. ❞**

There are traditional cheeses in every region of France, and traditional *pâtisseries* as well – the *canneles* of Bordelais, the *brioches* of La Vendée, the *gâteaux* Basques of the Pyrenées Atlantiques, the *tartes aux groseilles* of Bar-le-Duc, the *calissons* (little almond cakes) of Aix-en-Provence. There is even a little shop in St. Emilion that sells macaroons made to the same recipe since 1620.

Food is no exception to the general rule that fashion dictates everything. Nouvelle cuisine is the apotheosis of art in cooking; tiny pieces of food in a beautiful pattern – food for the eye rather than for the stomach – a triumph of style over substance. It intellectualises an essential primal function – one must eat to live, indeed, but one must live to discuss, and so food too must be worthy of analysis.

At a business conference, two French male colleagues talked together for over half an hour, not about sport or work, but about the mushrooms they had picked during the summer and how they ate them and with what sauce. Particular stress was placed on some very rare mushrooms which one of the delegates had found on a mountainside in Corsica and on the cream sauce that had accompanied them.

On the other hand, there is a lack of refinement about some French food that others find repellent. They not only eat any and every part of an animal, they take no trouble to hide which part it is. The British and the Americans mince up the toenails, genitals, brains, tails and ears of cows, pigs and sheep, turning them into unidentifiable products called 'burgers', 'brawn', 'haslet' or 'luncheon meat'. The French call a pig's foot *'un pied de porc'* and slap it on a tray with all the rest of the much-prized *charcuterie*.

The gibes historically hurled at the French for eating snails, frogs' legs and garlic are ineffective. The French know how to cook, serve and eat all three. Stomachs may quail at the snail, but the melted butter will be the finest in the world. Frogs' legs may seem to provide little in the way of sustenance, but they will be exquisitely arranged on the plate.

> **Stomachs may quail at the snail, but the melted butter will be the finest in the world.**

Drinking

Only the inhabitants of Luxembourg drink more than the French, who consume 15.5 litres of pure alcohol per head per year. In Normandy and Brittany vast quantities of cider pour down French throats and on to French livers – always a source of concern.

Beer is popular throughout France. The wealthy are fond of whisky, especially malt whisky which has special cachet. In south-west France, along the cosmopolitan coast, Gin Fizz is quaintly advertised in bars, a relic of older days. Pastis, Byrrh, and other apéritifs still have their devotees. But it is wine that makes the French world go round. The French *know* about wine. (They should do; they imbibe, combined with water, an ever-increasing amount of wine at mealtimes from a tender age.) Whatever the Spanish, the Germans, the Australians or the Californians may say, the French know that theyproduce the best wine in the world. Visitors to the University of Wine at Château Suze-la-Rousse or the Museum of Wine in Bordeaux tiptoe past the exhibits with more reverence than would be seen in Notre Dame.

> **"Visitors to the Museum of Wine in Bordeaux tiptoe past the exhibits with more reverence than would be seen in Notre Dame."**

A family of vegetarians, invited to dine with a French family in Bordeaux, were treated to a seven-course meal, every course of which was cheese. But there was a different bread to go with each cheese and, most importantly, a different wine to go with each duo. The meal was wonderful, each course superbly distinguished from the others; a '*grand vin*' here, a '*petit vin*' there. And the guests awoke the next morning with no after-effects.

> **After a banquet, the French President of the Board of Trade addressed guests for 10 minutes on the glories of the wines that had accompanied their meal.**

After a banquet, the French President of the Board of Trade addressed guests for a full 10 minutes, not on the economy or international trade or tariffs and duties, but on the glories of the wines that had accompanied their meal. He dwelled at length on the '78 de la Tour and the '55 Sauternes. He reviewed the experience in which they had all shared, and then led the assembled gathering in an act of bibulous worship.

What is sold where

Both men and women in France like to make a ceremony of shopping. Where others see it as a chore, especially something as humdrum and everyday as buying food, the French turn the whole thing into a cross between a drama and a pilgrimage.

French housewives set off with their wicker baskets and string bags to visit the *boulangerie*, *poissonnerie*, *pâtisserie*, *boucherie* and *fruiterie*. They prod, sniff, taste and generally assault whatever is on sale preparatory to buying it. To do anything less would be an insult to the trader. As they near their selection, an earnest discussion takes place between customer and shopkeeper, ultimately involving everyone within earshot – another of the much-loved French debates. The one knows what she wants; the other knows what she should have. Eventually an agreement is reached.

> **❝Housewives prod, sniff, taste and generally assault whatever is on sale preparatory to buying it. To do anything less would be an insult to the trader. ❞**

The French may have the largest, best-stocked supermarkets in the world outside the United States (and increasingly shop in them) but they also like to make their shops as specialised as possible. It is never necessary to ask 'Do you sell such-and-such?' It is perfectly obvious what any French shop sells, because it only sells one thing. Florists don't sell fruit, pharmacies don't sell sandwiches or CDs, *pâtisseries* don't sell bowls of soup.

The ultimate in specialisation is to be found in French butchers' shops. Here the discerning buyer has to make his or her way to shops that sell only red meat, only horse meat, only pork and pig products, only poultry. To obtain the ingredients for an English steak and kidney pie could take all day.

Health & Hygiene

Understandably, given their eating and drinking habits, the French view every ailment as a by-product of liver dysfunction. Colds, blisters, varicose veins, mumps, baldness, fallen arches – all are attributed to liver trouble. The cure for everything therefore, is to drink more Badoît, Evian, Perrier, Vichy, St. Yorre, Vittel – to flush out the offending organ. If this fails, the entire system has to be purged, and that means employing the French panacea – suppositories. The suppository is to the French what the cup of tea is to the English, useless as a treatment, but a great comfort in time of need.

The French believe in the expert. If you have a back pain in France, you go to see a back doctor. If you have a cough, you go to a chest specialist. If you have earache, you go to an expert on ears. (In rural areas this may pose problems, so there are large parts of France

> **The suppository is to the French what the cup of tea is to the English, useless as a treatment, but a great comfort in time of need.**

where treatment is still a matter for the wise older members of the family.) Since no one doctor has a monopoly on a person's illnesses, diseases and debilities, each patient is the custodian of his or her own medical records, which they take around with them to any doctor they visit. Averagely healthy citizens may, therefore, never see the same doctor twice, but they can give you chapter and verse on their medical histories, and thus have far more control over their own health and treatment.

Unless a French person is seriously ill, he or she is far more likely to go to a pharmacist than to a doctor. The pharmacist listens to the customer's self-diagnosis and then suggests what pills or potions should be taken. The work and effects of these drugs will be carefully described in great detail and the dosage recorded in clear, neat handwriting on the label. It is impossible to nip into a chemist's for a couple of painkillers without getting a complete rundown on The Work of the Aspirin.

66 **The French are not afraid of normal body odours, which they regard as natural.** 99

Hygiene

The French are not afraid of normal body odours – such smells they regard as natural. They have a saying: 'Don't be afraid of the microbes'. They regard the American obsession with hygiene as prissy. An average French family of four uses only one bar of soap a month.

To their minds, to cover up the stench of the body with deodorants is to make a pathetic attempt to defy the force of nature. The smell of a hot human being is a natural aphrodisiac to the French. They associate the smell as part of the overall sexual experience. Only the brave tourist travels in a crowded train from Paris to Nice in August.

It is not for nothing that the French are the world's leading *parfumeurs* – Christian Dior, Guérlain, Lancôme, Chanel, Madame Rochas. They see nothing incompatible in this. It is one thing to worship the smell of the human body and quite another to make billions of euros a year out of small phials of liquid that attempt to disguise it.

Systems

There is neither time nor place for the mediocre in the lives of the French. Services must be useless (grounds for complaint, argument, and possibly revolution) or excellent (grounds for sustained paeans of self-congratulation).

After limping along with a quaint and romantic telephone system for 50 years, the French decided they

> **❝ Services must be either useless or excellent – there is no place for the mediocre. ❞**

wanted a modern one in 1970, and by 1980 they had one of the best in the world: phones are fitted about five minutes after they are ordered.

Transport

The French, who are habitually late themselves, abhor lateness in public transport. If a train is two minutes late arriving at the most remote station in the Republic, testy phone calls are made up and down the line, and someone's peaked cap of authority is held up to ridicule. If a bus is late, the indignant passengers expect to be told why and are quite prepared to debate the strengths and weaknesses of the driver's excuse right there on the spot, even though it makes the bus even later.

> 66 The French are habitually late themselves but abhor lateness in public transport. 99

This obsession with punctuality can cause problems for passengers on the high speed train, the 'TGV'. As the train approaches a station, the conductor tells passengers how long the train will stop for, and this time is meticulously adhered to. It is thus a common sight on major French stations to see the automatic doors of the TGV closing before all descending passengers have got off and long before all ascending passengers have got on.

What is undeniable is that the French very sensibly made their country exactly the right size and shape for railways – medium-large, and square. There is none of the 'going-sideways' problem imposed on railways in Britain or Italy by the predominantly vertical shape of the country. There are none of the problems of size which bedevil Canadian, Russian or American railways where distances are so vast that a plane is bound to be a quicker method of travel. So the French have their TGV and their world records. It is fair and correct to expect the best and be furiously disappointed if it isn't forthcoming.

Although admitting that they have a role to play in allowing private, commercial and visiting vehicles to move about France, the French see their roads primarily as a means of connecting one town of great cultural and historical importance with a neighbouring town (of similar importance). This enables mayors and other civic dignatories easy access to each other for receptions, dinners, wine tastings.

Brown signs beside all the autoroutes warn drivers not of approaching junctions or hazards, but of approaching pine forests, oyster beds, châteaux, geese farms and mountains. Multi-coloured

> **66 French roads enable mayors and other civic dignatories easy access to each other for receptions, dinners, wine tastings. 99**

signs on all main roads alert drivers to approaching hotels, swimming pools, tennis courts, restaurants and historic churches. The French believe that, in order to arrive, one must travel hopefully.

France has far more internal air routes than are needed. Some of the routes are so short that there's scarcely time to tell passengers what action to take in anticipation of 'an emergency'. If time allows, however, they consider it essential to serve champagne on the flight, so that if there were to be 'an emergency', at least it would happen in style.

Education

The problems of attempting to change the education system in France reveal an essential truth about the French – you can change the superstructure, but you can't change the way the people behave.

After the student riots of 1968 all but the most diehard agreed that changes had to be made. A whole series of reforms were embarked on: mixed ability classes, an end to the separation of the academically gifted into special schools, more informality in teacher/pupil relationships.

66 The main aim of the educational reforms was 'a new Republican idealism', which was no different from the old Republican idealism. 99

None of it worked, because the main aim of all these reforms was 'a new Republican idealism', no different from the old Republican idealism. All that happened was that standards allegedly dropped.

The Government didn't mind about the worsening of standards in mathematics, science and technology, but it took a poor view of a drop in standards of knowledge of history (the story of France) and litera-

70

ture (the stories of France). The only popular educational reform during some 20 years was the creation of councils in all secondary schools – democratic governing boards composed of parents, pupils, teachers, Ministry officials and local bigwigs. These have quite happily fed the French hunger for debate without achieving anything.

The battle in French education has always been to wrest control from central government. Until the 1980s it was necessary to

> **66** Schools are so big that two teachers once met on holiday and were amazed to discover that they taught at the same school. **99**

get ministerial permission from Paris to hold a student dance in Grenoble or Bordeaux or Toulouse or any other French university.

Some independence has been won. Today, despite the imposition of a national curriculum which ensures that every child everywhere covers identical ground, French schools are permitted to decide for themselves how to spend 10% of their teaching time. They tend not to. It is the old story of the French shedding blood and laying down their lives to gain some essential freedom and then not knowing what to do with it.

French schools and universities are big. So big, that two teachers once met on holiday and were amazed to find that they taught at the same school. But this is not so surprising because education for teachers and pupils is very much a nose-to-the-grindstone affair.

All that matters is the famous *baccalauréat*, the end of school examination, the greatest French obsession of them all. Some parents are prepared to lie, bribe, cheat so that their children succeed in '*le bac*'. It is the essential qualification, for those who pass have proved that they are cultured, and those who fail are thought to be condemned to a life '*au chômage*', 'on the dole'. And yet the *bac*, is not an end in itself, merely a step to a decade or two at university. It often seems as if the French seek to collect degrees as others collect stamps or beer mats.

> 66 It often seems as if the French seek to collect degrees as others collect stamps or beer mats. 99

Law

This is yet another example of the French adherence to logic and discussion as a means of structuring life. The entire French legal system is based on an arbitrational rather than an adversarial model, with an intensive investigation under a judge's supervision before a case comes to court. The problem is that the number of examining magistrates has not increased since 1967, so the workload has become impossible.

In any legal dispute it is not a question of proving one side right and the other wrong, it is a question of arriving at the truth. In property deals, one lawyer can act for both buyer and seller because his or her role is simply to make sure that the deal is conducted fairly and legally. The lawyer is not there to help either side win, or to extort more money from the buyer, or to persuade the seller to drop the price (though he or she may suggest either of these moves if the deal is proving difficult). The system is based instead on the assumptions that:

a) we are all reasonable people
b) we all know what we want from this deal
c) dishonesty is not on the agenda

The French hold fast to these assumptions despite massive evidence to the contrary on all three counts.

Crime & Punishment

The French police in whatever form – *gendarmes*, CRS (riot police), national police – have an unchallenged and widely held reputation for being tough, vain and heavily corrupt. So the French are not shocked when this is proved to be the case.

There is a most revealing scene in a French film called *Le Cop* between a keen provincial policeman and a worldly wise city cop. The provincial thinks it's his duty to catch every criminal around and, seizing a man who has snatched a woman's bag, brings him back in triumph to the *gendarmerie*. Here the worldly

73

cop takes over and interviews the bag snatcher: "You picked up the bag in the street, didn't you? You were going to hand it in to the nearest police station at the first available opportunity, weren't you?" The bemused criminal nods. "Fine," he is told, "sign this statement and if the bag hasn't been claimed in a year you can come and collect it." The bag snatcher legs it. The provincial cop is infuriated, but his worldly colleague explains "This memo from HQ says that our district has the worst record of larceny in police history. It says we must take every step to ensure it's reduced." The step taken is simply to cover up crime. It doesn't matter that this is a total fraud. The important thing is that, on paper, they will have obeyed the memo from headquarters and will also have accepted life as it really is – with a shrug.

> **The average *gendarme* is more concerned with fighting paperwork than fighting crime.**

The average *gendarme* is more concerned with fighting paperwork than fighting crime. Thus tax evasion, illicit gambling, black-market dealing, petty theft and vagrancy are 'not serious' enough to sully the records, but they make exceptions for serious matters such as rape, murder, arson and assault.

Occasionally nothing is worth bothering about. In a tiny *gendarmerie* in a little village in south-west France some days the local *gendarmes* play marbles or *boules*; at other times they listen to dance music or blow up balloons for their children. Every day they close the *gendarmerie* for two hours at lunchtime, while delicious smells waft from the kitchen at the back. Every evening they are to be seen sipping apéritifs on the terrace. If you knock on their door to report a mugging, they are much put out, but will helpfully give you the phone number of the *gendarmerie* in St. Jean de Luz, a few miles away. The locals are not in the least disturbed by any of this.

It would be a mistake, however, to underestimate the French police. If they take a dislike to you, they can hold you in the cells for up to 24 hours without bringing any charge. This is known as 'detained under surveillance'.

Crime statistics suggest that the French are about as criminal as the English and far less so than the Americans. But every nation has its own speciality: the French are not much interested in car theft or indecent assault, but they do like larceny and murder. They have a very low rate for attempted murder and a high rate for successfully concluded murder. It seems that when a French person sets out to kill someone, they make a good job of it. This is especially true of the *crime passionnel*, which is accorded special status, passion being a perfectly understandable motive.

> **The French are not much interested in car theft or indecent assault, but they do like larceny and murder.**

Government & Bureaucracy

The French like government intervention in their lives. In their eyes, the State not only has a role to play in the everyday life of the country, the State is France (as are cooking, wine, women, the land, Paris, culture, children, liberty-equality-fraternity, and the right to park on a pedestrian crossing).

State intervention is something to be proud of, not something to avoid. By the side of new roads huge placards proclaim the partnership between the State, the region and the department which has paid for the improvements. The Paris subway system is a monument to state planning – it is flawlessly integrated, the Métro linking with the main railway, linking in turn with the Aéroport Charles de Gaulle.

As soon as the technology exists, the French put it to use. There is little sense of 'We know we can do it, but can we afford it?' Instead, they believe that if they can do it, they must make sure they can afford it.

66 The way the French deal with bureaucracy is to accept that it is necessary, and indeed proper, but find ways to circumvent it. 99

All this means that bureaucracy flourishes in France – in post offices, railway stations, customs sheds, town halls, tourist offices, *gendarmeries*, schools. The way the French deal with it is to accept that it is necessary, and indeed proper, but find ways to circumvent it.

The French have always affirmed their right to ignore rules (which are always 'petty' when they disagree with them).

Politics

The current French Constitution was drafted in the knowledge that a lurch towards tyranny afflicts France once every generation. This is counterbalanced by a delight in playing with democracy and having lots and lots of tiny political parties, who represent small farmers, small shopkeepers, small fishermen. Most of these parties have a mayfly existence, fluttering around the National Assembly for a few weeks or months until they crash out of existence.

> **66 The current French Constitution was drafted in the knowledge that a lurch towards tyranny afflicts France once every generation. 99**

Until recently, the French enjoyed a system that deliberately built confusion and complication into their constitution. Whereas the president was elected for seven years, members of the National Assembly were elected for five. This guaranteed times when president and parliament were out of step – a situation the French quaintly called *'cohabitation'*. The president is now elected for five years. Nonetheless, *cohabitation* still flourishes, for presidential and parliamentary elections are held at different times.

France may no longer be a world power of the first significance, but French politicians show no signs of behaving as if that were true. They took no notice of the world's outrage at their plan to resume nuclear tests on the Mururoa Atoll. Only a truly great nation could have so many enemies.

> **All French politicians are expected to look smart. The French electorate would never allow any government to intervene in their lives if it were shabbily dressed.**

The French like their politicians to be bold and visionary. They can forgive any misdemeanour if it is big enough. This is just as well because it is an unwritten law of the French Constitution that each new government should reveal an appalling scandal perpetrated by the one before.

All French politicians are also expected to look smart, whatever their shape or age. They look smart because power itself is chic, attractive, seductive, and one should dress to look the part. The French electorate would never allow any government to intervene in their lives if it were shabbily dressed.

As to the private lives of their representatives, the French cannot understand the problem other nations have when their politicians are discovered engaged in a sexual liaison. It is expected that all male French politicians have mistresses or lovers. Indeed, once a French politician is known to have a lover, he or she can count on more votes.

Business

The French have mastered the art of invisible work. Whereas some nations parade the sweat and grime of industrial and constructional life, the French keep all this hidden. It is as though having to work is incompatible with the notion that the French have discovered the secret of the good life.

They take their work seriously, and conduct it in the formal manner that dictates every aspect of their lives. Behind the scenes (jackets off, ties undone, Gauloise on the lip), all may be friendly and informal. But in the front office even if they had been calling each other by their first names for decades, etiquette dictates that they should call each other '*Monsieur* X', '*Madame* Y'. The French use '*Monsieur*' in conversations

> **It is as though having to work is incompatible with the notion that the French have discovered the secret of the good life.**

in the workplace in much the same way that the English used 'Sir' 70 years ago: "Did you know, *Monsieur*, that…"

And every morning French business colleagues have to shake hands with each other. Everything must be *comme il faut* (right and proper) before any attempt to work can be made.

Once work is under way, there is a lot of good sense in French practice. Reports within an office as

79

to how well a member of staff is performing are compiled not only by the subject's line manager or seniors, but also by the employees on the lower rungs of the office ladder, who have a different but important perspective on performance.

> **The French see graphology as a fully fledged science, revealing character. Secretly, though, they must bless the invention of the word processor.**

There are, however, some strange aspects to the way French businesses recruit their office staff. Graphology (the analysis of handwriting) is regarded as an essential assessment tool. If a French person takes a dislike to your handwriting, he may well cancel appointments with you, may even refuse to employ you. The French see graphology as a fully fledged science, revealing character (or lack of it). Secretly, though, they must bless the invention of the word processor.

Time keeping

Despite their strong belief in protocol, manners and the proprieties of life, the French are almost always late for work, for appointments, for interviews, etc. They have their own special idea of what constitutes being 'on time'. It means 'being within 15 minutes of the appointed hour'. In their eyes, therefore, they are never late.

Decision making

Sit a group of British managers down to solve a problem and they will make an honest attempt, eventually coming up with a solution, no matter how unsuitable. Faced with the same problem, French managers will enjoy the discussion, move smartly off at several tangents, and end up with a totally new problem to discuss, to their great satisfaction. This is how they arrive at the latest ideas, fashions, gadgets, kitchen utensils...

The way it's done

The sense of propriety among business colleagues means that they very rarely invite each other home to dinner, or for a drink. The idea of inviting someone from the office for a casual glass of wine, in casual clothes, is unthinkable. Indeed, the French don't really have a word for 'casual'. The nearest they get to it is *decontracte*, or the cruder *sans-gêne*, literally 'without constraint'.

> 66 The French don't have a word for 'casual'. The nearest they get to it is 'without constraint'. 99

The uniform business suit is not commonly worn to work. The French dress with the same flair and imagination that accompanies all that they do. Jackets and trousers of bright and unusual designs and colours (even in banks) are the rule, and dress is no indication of status in the French business world. This does not mean that they are not all intensely conscious of whose outfit is the smartest, the most stylish. *Egalité* may rule, but some are more *égal* than others. This is apparent in the French attitude to working women. It was only in 1945 that they received the vote, and as late as 1965 it was legally possible for a husband to forbid his wife to work. Women now account for some 48% of the French workforce, but few are to be found in the key positions in industry and big business – despite their high profile in politics from time to time.

66 The romantic, inaccurate view of the French is that they are a nation of entrepreneurs. 99

The romantic, inaccurate view of the French is that they are a nation of entrepreneurs – small blacksmiths, small builders, small *notaires*. It was widely held that if a motorist broke down in the most remote French village, the local blacksmith would be able to repair the car, even if it meant hammering out a new fuel pump from a chunk of solid metal. In fact, small businesses are increasingly the exception rather than the rule. The French are happy to accept the notion of the large company, for the large company can afford vision and experimentation. It is far more glamorous and thus gives its workforce a feeling of notoriety. French workers have a pride in their job because they are aware of what they are giving to the community and to France.

The workers, united

The French are as conservative with a small 'c' as they are socialist with a small 's'. This ingrained political schizophrenia allows them to have remarkably cordial industrial relations in a country with hundreds of thousands of communist voters – both the sort that sell left-wing tracts at street corners, and the sort that live in fine houses and write the tracts.

On the whole, the French don't believe in trade unions. Less than 10% of the workforce are members (compared with 29% in the U.K.), and the figure falls steadily year by year.

This lack of interest boils down to two things: that French people don't like joining anything, and that the main unions are usually in dispute with each other (an 'us and us', rather than an 'us and them' problem).

> **The French are as conservative with a small 'c' as they are socialist with a small 's'.**

French industry is run by cunning, imaginative men (and one or two women) who make work seem like a pleasant interlude between morning coffee and evening apéritifs. They put rest-rooms in their offices and factories, establish flexi-time, allow workers to take a few minutes' break whenever they need to, and even let them finish work for the week on a Thursday if they've already reached their productivity targets. Trade unions wither in the face of such unfair and reasonable onslaughts.

Obsessions

To the French there is little point in living unless one is obsessed. They are obsessed with the Tour de France, the state of their health, the National Lottery, the *bac*, the meaning of life, barricades and revolutions, and all that is inherently theirs.

> **To the French there is little point in living unless one is obsessed.**

Watch the way they play *boules* – the muttering through the Gitanes, the peering through half-shut eyes, the wiping of sweat from the brow (only the French could break into a sweat simply by throwing a small metal ball in the air), the grunting of joy or rage as the point is won or lost, the handshakes all round at the end of every three-minute game. If an innocent pastime can produce such dedication, then what of codes of honour, truth, patriotism, duty and the correct temperature at which to thicken a sauce?

Language & Ideas

The French language is what binds the French together. In the old days, France was divided into regions that spoke different tongues, like Breton, Languedoc, Flemish. Almost every area had its own *patois*. This was seen as a threat to French unity, and in schools any child who spoke the forbidden *patois* was given a bean. The bean passed from miscreant to miscreant during the day, and at the end of the day the child in possession of the bean was caned.

No other nation has fought so hard to preserve its language. An entire academy (the Académie française) works ceaselessly to ensure its purity, examining every word to make sure it is acceptable. New words that have crept into use are ruthlessly plucked out.

> **❝ The Académie française works ceaselessly to ensure the purity of the language, examining every word to make sure it is acceptable. ❞**

The fad of franglais has upset many purists but been difficult to stamp out. In business and technical terminology *'le cash-flow'*, *'le design'*, *'le pipeline'* appalled Mitterrand (President from 1981–1995): "Must we give orders to our computers in English?" he demanded. An attempt was made to render franglais unnecessary by creating French substitutes. *'Un oil-rig'* became *'un appareil de forage en mer'*. The attempt was quickly abandoned.

When de Gaulle died, Noel Coward was asked what he thought the good General and God would find to talk about in Heaven. Coward replied: "That depends on how good God's French is."

Words to the world

The linguistic bequest of the French to the world has been indispensable. What sort of romance could be conducted without a *tête-à-tête*, a *rendezvous* with the right *ambiance*, a *frisson* or two, some *badinage*, the odd *nuance* and some *risquée* repartee?

What sort of a war could anyone conduct without *sabotage*, *manœuvres*, the odd *massacre*, many and frequent *mêlées*, bags of *esprit de corps*, a little *espionage*, *liaison*, and ultimately *détente*?

> **66 How could we show that we were out of our *milieu* if we couldn't make *gaffes* and *faux pas* to show that we were thoroughly *gauche*? 99**

What sort of poise could anyone achieve without being *suave* and *soigné*? And what sort of political excitement or intrigue could there be without *coups d'état*, *laisser-faire*, *faits accomplis*, *volte-face* and *carte blanche*?

How could we show that we were out of our *milieu* if we couldn't make *gaffes* and *faux* pas to show that we were thoroughly *gauche*? What would we eat in a *restaurant*, a *buffet*, or a *café* without *casseroles*, *fricassées*, *hors-d'œuvre*, *soufflés*, *vols au vent*, *escalopes*, *consommés*, *pâté*, *terrines*, *éclairs*, *croissants*, *omelettes*, *gâteaux*, *mousses* and *sauces*...? And wouldn't everything simply be *passé* were it not for the *avant-garde*?

The Authors

Nick Yapp spent his first night in France in a barn near Calais docks in 1961. Since then he has loved the French for their music, wine, space, and 15 species of onions. When he sits outside a café in a small French town on a sunny day, sipping strong coffee, he feels he has made a success of his life. When he gets the bill and sees what this success has cost him, a little of the euphoria evaporates – but he returns the next day.

He used to be a teacher, but escaped to become a writer and broadcaster. In his dreams he lives in a villa on the cliffs south of Biarritz. In reality, he lives in a flat in south-east London.

Michel Syrett, French on his mother's side, visits France regularly as a business commentator, lecturer and journalist. His French has benefited from eulogising in business circles about the perfect style with which the Nuits St. George cohabits with the *fromage*, while making an intellectual evaluation of the *fois gras*. He finds this a pleasure as, being French in his soul, he values food as a spiritual experience.

The Germans

The Germans like things that work. This is fundamental. A car or a washing machine which breaks down six months after purchase is not a nuisance, it's a breach of the social contract.

The Spanish

Anyone attempting to understand the Spanish must first of all recognise the fact that they do not consider anything important except total enjoyment. If it is not enjoyable it will be ignored.

The English

Stoicism, the capacity to greet life's vicissitudes with cheerful calm, is an essential ingredient of Englishness. The English, who suspect that all foreigners tend to over-react and 'make a meal of things', will warm to you instantly if you display understated good humour in the face of adversity.

The Americans

When asked in a survey what they notice first in a potential mate, the answer from both men and women was 'hair'. Having good hair is more important than having a college education or a happy family.

The Italians

Italians grow up knowing that they have to be economical with the truth. All other Italians are, so if they didn't play the game they would be at a serious disadvantage.

The Swiss

The Swiss say about money: "You don't talk about it, you just have it." There is even a law supporting this: Swiss employment contracts prohibit workers disclosing their salaries to colleagues. Job advertisements are similarly prevented from stating the salary on offer.

Comments on other titles

On the series:

"If I were a cabaret artist or stand up comedian, I'd just get up and read these books to the audience as they would bring the house down." Reviewer of *Het Parool*, Holland

The Americans:

"Stunning observations about American culture that not even most Americans would realize are true." Reader from Boston, USA

The Aussies:

"One gem of a book. Compulsory reading for anyone interested in visiting Australia or living there. Don't look like a stunned mullet, read the guide." Reader from Germany

The Greeks:

"Hilariously accurate. I laughed so much as it really does sum up the Greeks and their wonderful mentality so perfectly."
Reader from Corfu

The Icelanders:

"Witty and fun to read, you get to learn some really incredible facts as well as their quirky habits. Essential reading for anyone planning a trip there or remotely interested in the place." Reader from London

Xenophobe's® guides

The Americans	The Poles
The Aussies	The Russians
The Austrians	The Scots
The Belgians	The Spanish
The Californians	The Swedes
The Canadians	The Swiss
The Chinese	The Welsh
The Czechs	
The Danes	
The Dutch	
The English	**Xenophobe's®** lingo learners
The French	
The Germans	❝Speak the lingo by speaking English.❞
The Greeks	
The Icelanders	
The Irish	French
The Israelis	German
The Italians	Greek
The Japanese	Italian
The Kiwis	Spanish

Oval Books

5 St John's Buildings Canterbury Crescent London SW9 7QH

We like to hear from our readers.
Please send us your views on our books and
we will publish them as appropriate on our
web site: ovalbooks.com.

Oval Books also publish the best-selling
Bluffer's Guide® series –
see www.ovalbooks.com

Both series can be bought via Amazon or directly
from us, Oval Books through our web site
www.ovalbooks.com or by contacting us.

Oval Books charges the full cover price
for its books (because they're worth it) and
£2.00 for postage and packing on the first
book. Buy a second book or more and
postage and packing will be entirely FREE.

To order by post please fill out the accompanying
order form and send to:
Oval Books
5 St John's Buildings
Canterbury Crescent
London SW9 7QH

cheques should be made payable to: Oval Books

or phone us on +44 (0)20 7733 8585
or visit our web site at: www.ovalbooks.com

Payment may be made by Visa or Mastercard and orders are
dispatched as soon as the card details and mailing address are
received. If the mailing address is not the same as the card holder's
address it is necessary to give both.

Oval Books